A POETIC TRIBUTE

HER NOBEL VOICE
Women Laureates of the Nobel Peace Prize
1905-2014

Her Nobel Voice

*Women Laureates of the
Nobel Peace Prize*

1905 - 2014

Andrea M. Owens

Shoestring Book Publishing

Her Nobel Voice

Women Laureates of the Nobel Peace Prize

1905 – 2014

Paperback Edition

ISBN: 978-1-943974-01-6

Library of Congress Control Number: 2016934035

Published by: Shoestring Book Publishing. Maine, USA

Layout and design by Shoestring Book Publishing

For information address:
shoestringpublishing4u@gmail.com
www.shoestringbookpublishing.com

Contents

Path to Peace

Authentic humanity -

Her collective soul,

Relentlessly she seeks -

To find and follow her path to peace.

Artist- Noredin Morgan- Poet, A.M. Owens

Introduction

Photo courtesy of Harper's Bazaar

Were it not for a friend and influencer of Alfred Nobel known as Baroness Bertha Sophie Felicita von Suttner, in all likelihood there would not have been a Nobel Prize for Peace Award.

In 1911, the Baroness became a member of the advisory council of the Carnegie Peace Foundation indirectly linking me to this endeavor as a former employee of TIAA-CREF, a financial services provider which began with a one million dollar philanthropic gift from Andrew Carnegie in 1918 for purpose of providing professors in the United States retirement services. I too, was educated as a teacher in the area of music education but never fulfilled the short term purpose of my education. My implausible and encircling path has brought me here.

My interest in this project began without my conscious consent in May of 2008 by way of happenstance with an all inclusive invitation to meet the newly appointed CEO/President of TIAA-CREF,

Roger W. Ferguson whose words regarding a need to address global students inspired my curious investigative research, ideas, and whose understanding of the process of leadership development focused and challenged my souls quest to discover the full power of my poetic voice, influence, and potential for which I am eternally grateful.

For the immeasurable creative contribution of the female race to love, bear, nurture, protect, encourage, support, educate, inspire, and instill a legacy of human compassion throughout the ages; among these my homage and poetic tribute to the sixteen female recipients of the Nobel Peace Prize, 1905-2014. I humbly dedicate my thoughts and poetic verse to each in sacred gratitude to their historical contribution as great spirits of courage, intellect, and sacrifice toward humanity's path to peace.

Andrea M. Owens

BENEATH THE VEIL

Beneath her head -

she carries a mind of boundless imagination

Beneath her breast -

sings a heart of love's compassion

Beneath her hands -

she holds the weight of truth and justice

Beneath her waist -

she bears a garden that brings forth humanity

Beneath her feet -

she walks the earth in wisdom and harmony

Beneath the veil -

her triumphant silent song awaits its release

A melody of unity and peace that will heal the nations -

Beneath the veil

A.M. Owens

A POETIC TRIBUTE

HER NOBEL VOICE
Women Laureates of the Nobel Peace Prize
1905-2014

Malala Yousafzai

Photo courtesy of Harper's Bazaar

Awarded the Nobel Peace Prize – 2014

*Prize in equal share with Kailash Satyarthi

"For their struggle against suppression of children and young people and for the right of all children to education."

"One child, one teacher, one pen, and one book can change the world."

Malala Yousafzai*

"One humanity, one wisdom, one story,
and one song to light one path to peace."

A.M. Owens

Ellen Johnson Sirleaf, Leymah Gbowee & Tawakel Karman

| Ellen | Leymah | Tawakel |

Photo courtesy of Harper's Bazaar

Awarded the Nobel Peace Prize – 2011

"For their non-violent struggle for the safety of women and for women's rights to full participation in peace-building work."

"Future generations will judge us not by what we say, but by what we do."

Ellen Johnson Sirleaf

"Activism is something that no one can fake... that anger is what is propelling you to further action."

Leymah Gbowee

"Peace does not mean just to stop wars, but also to stop oppression and injustice."

Tawakel Karman

<u>Peace Building</u>

First bridge I will build up and take into my hand—

This is the first bridge.

The first bridge between -

Paradise and great lands.

A.M. Owens

Wangari Muta Maathai

Photo courtesy of Harper Bazaar

Awarded the Nobel Peace Prize – 2004

"For her contribution to sustainable development,
democracy and peace."

For me, one of the major reasons to move beyond just the planting of trees--to look at the causes of a problem. We often preoccupy ourselves with the symptoms, whereas if we went to the root cause of the problems, we would be able to overcome the problems once and for all.

Wangari Muta Maathai

Nature's Song

Sweetly sing my souls great music -

From root of tree to branch of vine.

On life's path the storm clouds gather -

Yet in her calm, a rainbow sky.

A.M. Owens

Shirin Ebadi

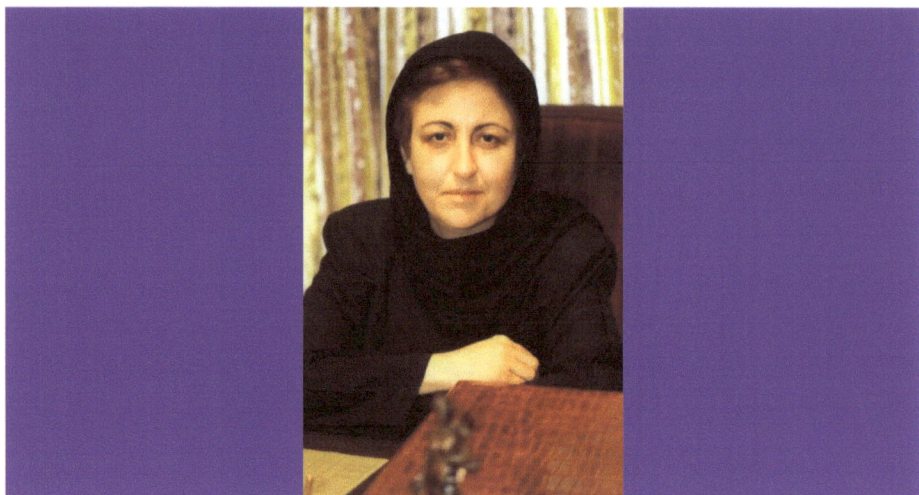

Photo courtesy of Harper's Bazaar

Awarded the Nobel Peace Prize – 2003

"For her efforts for democracy and human rights. She has focused especially on the struggles for the rights of women and children."

"We demand a non-violent world where human security is the basis of our common global security.
People have the right to live in a world where the basic needs of all peoples are addressed.
No more military attacks. No more war."

Shirin Ebadi

One Accord

Long discouraged in despair -

Earthly service to sustain,

Courage to paint the world with care.

Wash away root source of pain -

Mercy code found sea to shores.

Nations put down every sword,

Noble love guards and endures -

Them to us to one accord.

A.M. Owens

Jody Williams

Photo courtesy of Harper's Bazaar

Awarded the Nobel Peace Prize – 1997

"For her work for the banning and clearing of anti-personnel mines."

"For me, the difference between an 'ordinary' and 'extraordinary' person is not the title that a person might have, but what they do to make the world a better place."

Jody Williams

World of Good

There is greatness in each of us

but there is no shortcut to reaching its heights.

It's taking the long and winding road.

It's those mountains to climb -

It's experiencing the valley of despair.

It's staring fear in the face so long it has to back down

so you can walk over it.

It's understanding that the ordinary

can be extraordinary

when we unite our heads, hearts and hands

And it's a knowing that in daily serving each other -

We feed our divine nature,

so that together we can serve humanity.

And together create a world of good.

A.M. Owens

Rigobarta Menchu Tum

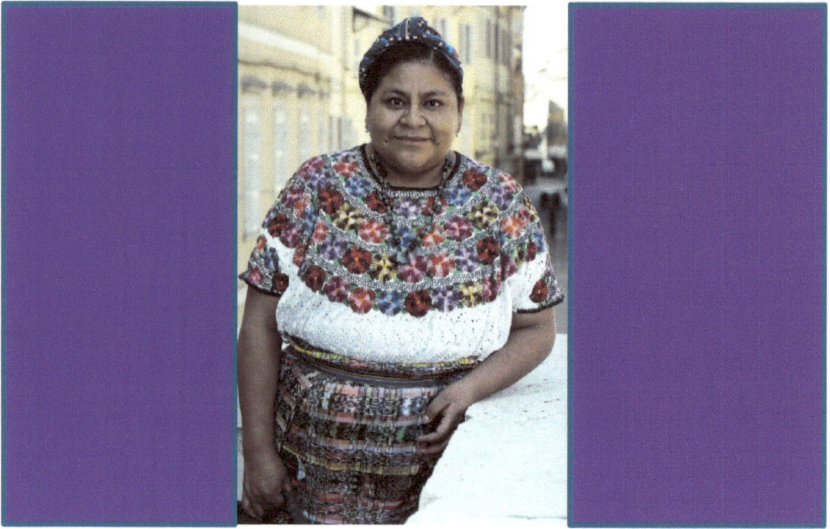

Photo courtesy of Harper's Bazaar

Awarded the Nobel Peace Prize – 1992

"In recognition of her work for social justice and ethno-culture reconciliation based on respect for the rights of indigenous peoples."

"We have learned that change cannot come through war. War is not a feasible tool to use in fighting against the oppression we face. War has caused more problems. We cannot embrace that path."

Rigobarta Menchu Tum

Peace in Amazing Grace

Songful wisdom angel's message -

Black swan in storm lays golden egg.

Faith rose to illumination -

Major and minor keys transposed,

Reconciliation sounding -

Common meters sacred chorus,

Great spiritual transformation -

Gathering human dignity,

Visions glory in redemption found -

Amazing grace in unity.

A.M. Owens

Aung San Suu Kyi

Photo courtesy of Harper's Bazaar

Awarded the Nobel Peace Prize – 1991

"For her non-violent struggle for democracy and human rights."

"The only real prison is fear,
and the only real freedom is freedom from fear."

Aung San Suu Kyi

"Freedom in peace is the key to unlock the chains of fear, and opens wide humanity's potential door."

A.M. Owens

Alva Murdal

Photo courtesy of Harper's Bazaar

Awarded the Nobel Peace Prize – 1982

Prize in equal share with Alfonso Garcia Robles *

"For her non-violent struggle for democracy and human rights."

A great amount has been talked and written about what constitutes a sufficient balance and what really is meant by the concepts of "balance" and "deterrence."

Alva Myrdal*

Point of Balance

"It is our time to be the catalyst, to transform culture and
consciousness at its root -

By honoring the full value, goodness and power of female force -
To create an ethical and spiritual balance that will heal all nations
and our planet.

This is the path of unity -

In relationship to, and sustainability of, humankind and earth herself -

For she is the core of creation."

A.M. Owens

Mother Teresa of Calcutta

Photo courtesy of Harper's Bazaar

Awarded the Nobel Peace Prize – 1979

"For her charity work"

"Kind words are short and easy to speak,
but their echoes are truly endless."

Mother Teresa of Calcutta

Echoes Song

Though shrouded in deep silence,

Arise, for spirits sing,

In dusty winds of living,

Victorious symbol rings.

Rings faint but journeys forward

Through forge of crooked paths.

Our skies are clothed in rainbows,

In tales of distant past -

Til' round the centuries turning

In one encircling grasp,

The song cannot be silenced -

The song its echoes last.

A.M. Owens

Betty Williams & Mairead Corrigan

Betty   **Mairead**

Photo courtesy of Harper's Bazaar

Awarded the Nobel Peace Prize – 1976

"For her work as a cofounder of Community of Peace People, an organization dedicated to promoting a peaceful resolution to the Troubles in Northern Ireland."

"The voice of women has a special role and a special soul force in the struggle for a nonviolent world."

Betty Williams

Force of Soul

"The goodness of a woman lies not in her timidity,
but in lending her bold collective voice in a call for a global
collaborative force toward actuating peace."

A.M. Owens

"If we want to reap the harvest of peace and justice in the future, we will have to sow seeds of nonviolence, here and now in the present."

Mairead Corrigan

"Sow potential, reap greatness."

A.M. Owens

Emily Greene Balch

Awarded the Nobel Peace Prize – 1946

"For being a lifetime advocate of the persecuted and oppressed."

"As the world community develops in peace, it will open up great untapped reservoirs in human nature."

Emily Greene Balch

All Heart

Heart room residing,

Nurture of nature living,

Human ground broken -

Break new ground.

Sown in common communion,

Equally watered potential transforms.

Reaping one community of peace,

Grateful hearted mutuality beings -

Open hearts door restored.

Earth home sustained,

Full heart known.

A.M. Owens

Jane Addams

Awarded the Nobel Peace Prize – 1931

"A school teacher and peace advocate,
influencing the later shape of the United Nations."

*"What after all has maintained the human race on this old globe-
Despite all the calamities of nature and all tragic failings of mankind-
If not faith, in new possibilities and courage to advocate them."*

Jane Addams

Faith in Possibilities

She had a song of unity and peace in her heart

Courage to step out of the boat

And a force of faith to walk on water.

A.M. Owens

Bertha Von Suttner

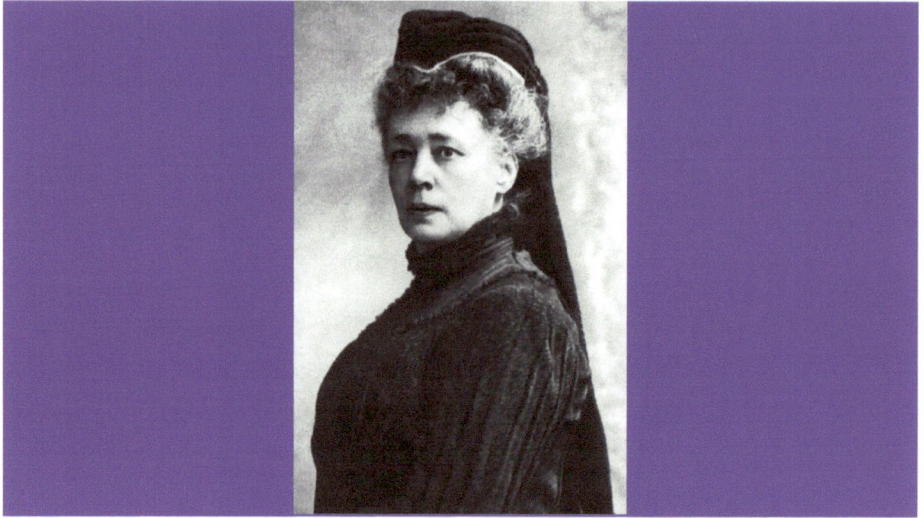

Photo courtesy of Harper's Bazaar

Baroness Bertha Sophie Felicita von Suttner*

Awarded the Nobel Peace Prize – 1905

"Peace activist and the first women to be awarded
the Noble Peace Prize"*

*"The message of the peace movement is not some fanciful dream
which is out of touch with the world—it is a message which embodies
the survival instinct of civilization."*

Bertha Von Suttner

Inner Room

Wandering steps in the halls of grace,

Seeking to find its hidden rooms.

Light plays her joy filled harmonies –

Wallpaper of ordered design.

Divine window curtain opens -

Equally seated

Potential transforms.

Table set full sustenance found,

Well-made bed where trials faith heals.

Sleep safe on the pillows of wisdom,

Dreamer's well-being music plays.

A.M. Owens

*(In 1911, Baroness Bertha Sophie Felicita von Suttner became a member of the advisory council of the Carnegie Peace Foundation).

Lady Peace

She was born to dream in music.

Born feeling angels cry,

She was born with faith in healing.

Born to dare to try,

She was born with strength and courage.

Born to question why,

She was born with secret insight.

Born to climb and fly,

She was born in full truths table

With compassion from above.

She was born to solve the riddle

Sound wisdoms' source—a dove.

She has journeyed to the answer

To make music from history's notes

Its chords to play sweet harmonies,

A song of peace she wrote.

She was born the unseen seer.

Born of poetic design,

She was born to serve humanity.

Born to love mankind.

A.M. Owens

Author's Biography

Andrea M. Owens was born in Saint Johnsbury, Vermont on September 1st, 1960 (late stage baby boomer) to Mack Owens and Jacquelyn (Golden) Owens.

Her Dad was born in Fountain, North Carolina on November 7th, 1930, twelve years to the day after Billy Graham, and so too became a pastor, not of a global ministry but a struggling home missionary starting Baptist churches in Canada and the Northeast following his ministerial training at what is now Welsh University in Nashville, TN.

Her Mom was born in Littleton, New Hampshire on February 16th 1936 and became a mother, homemaker and nurse but according to her nursing training evaluation, her strong suit was psychology. Her Mom met her Dad in Nashville where they were introduced by her Moms brother, Tom. Prior to giving birth to her first born child, Andrea's sister Rebecca, her Mom worked at Life & Casualty in Nashville, TN. (A life insurance company) as a clerk calculating eight thousand dividends every three months.

Along with her brother Randy, and two sisters, Becky & Brenda Andrea attended at least ten different schools prior to attending secondary school.

Being a 'preacher's kid' an abiding faith in a guiding force and deep sense of social justice developed. As a naturally gifted vocalist she began to sing publically in church as a soloist at the age of six. From the beginning, she was a high functioning introvert, curious, creative forming patterns in nature and spiritual thinking based on her belief framework, experiences, travel and independent studies. To this day she is emotionally sensitive to sound especially music and disturbed by violence.

Upon her completion of college as a music teacher in 1984 it was difficult to find work. She ended up working in the mailroom of a medical instrumentation company where her brother-in-law worked as a programmer. After 3 years, she was reviewing telecom billing and working as a receptionist.

Her next job was at Digital Equipment (DEC) where she was hired as a Telecom Analyst, which gave her a broad based foundation in IT and Marketing experience for the next six years. The next move was Fujitsu Network Switching, which only lasted two years. She made contact with a former DEC associate and started a small business as an overflow call center for Serif, Inc. She struggled with that for three years and ended up filing bankruptcy on or about 1998.

From there she joined mostly small IT start-ups in Account Management/Business Development roles where she met with repeated failure. By 2004 she was working as temporary administrative assistant for KNF&T Staffing Resources in Boston until her full time position with TIAA-CREF began in March of 2007. At last not a challenging role but she felt well-suited to the company's mission and the position provided stability for Andrea.

Then one day in May of 2008 everything changed. The new CEO arrived in the Waltham office to meet with the staff and everyone was included in the invitation. Roger met with a group of twenty or so including Andrea and talked about the challenges that lay ahead. Roger shared that several marketing executives recommended that TIAA needed to do something globally with higher education students. In that instant, she became inspired and alive in a way she never could have imagined and began to research that next day. She mentally mapped the history of TIAA beginning with 1918, and that of education in the U.S., looking for a global connection that would fit into a logical strategic direction for TIAA. She reached out to a few knowledgeable players asking probing questions that led her to google the UN website, where she learned the formation of the entity called the *Principles of Responsible Management Education* (PRME). This organization had already formed online training modules for Social Responsibility for global university students working on their master's degree.

Intuitively, she knew the answer was to piggy back on this technology with financial literacy modules and provide students with the ability to set up the financial portfolios while in college, later adding to make them portable through each career change until the age of retirement. She emailed her findings to Roger and he immediately replied, thank you. The infancy of the idea which she thought would give TIAA a global footprint in services, was actually something even bigger. Roger found ways to encourage her gift from afar so that in time she could fully link her critical thinking process to what her heart strings already knew intuitively.

Over the next three years, her ideas continued to flow freely of what else needed to be added to the plan (see LinkedIN accomplishments) as she would email internal executives her ideas. New organizations and initiatives formed. To her dismay she was not included, yet still she forged on. About five years went by in which time she began to write poetry that mirrored her harmonic vision. Creating poetry became her outlet for inclusion in the formation of the company's strategy, initiatives, programs and planning. Finally, the full vision of her intuition from the start was revealed to her. TIAA would be the catalyst to change everything by bringing together government, academia, industry, technology, and global philanthropic players to inspire the next generation of students everywhere to become socially responsible by empowering them to be part of a grand framework, a global sustainability model.

Her ever struggling and changing life's path, filled with seeming missteps, fit perfectly together like puzzle pieces slowly being put into place, leading to her authentic self and full potential. She became self-empowered by realizing her truth in purpose. She was not just a spiritual minded, musically inclined, introverted loner; her passion was peace.

Website: www.shestandsforall.com

Appendix: Information Links

1-	www.peacejam.org
2-	www.nobelwomensinitiative.org
3-	www.internationalwomensday.com
4-	www.unwomen.org
5-	www.nobelpeacecenter.org
6-	www.nobelprize.org
7-	www.peacefoundation.org.za
8-	www.edgbastonhigh.co.uk
9-	www.wisc.edu
10-	www.emu.edu
11-	http://smmpchs.com/
12-	www.sanauniv.net
13-	http://benedictine.edu
14-	http://ut.ac.ir
15-	www.harpersbazaar.co.uk
16-	http://www.uvm.edu/
17-	http://jhu.edu
18-	http://www.uh.edu
19-	www.nova.edu
20-	www.centersofcompassion.org
21-	http://tcd.academia.edu
22-	http://emu.edu
23-	http://uu.se
24-	www.motherteresafoundation.org.in
25-	http://brynmawr.edu
26-	http://rockford.edu
27-	www.tiaa-cref.org
28-	http://carnegiefoundation.org
29-	http://carnegieendowment.org
30-	http://womensworldbanking.org

Contact Information for the Cover Designer of

Her Nobel Voice

Women Laureates of the Nobel Peace Prize

1905 – 2014:

Samira
Blanco
Graphic Designer,
Deity Designz 978.242.5623
|
Deitydesignz@gmail.com
|
https://deitydesignz.carbonmade.com/

Are you inspired by *Her Nobel Voice*?

If so, please support Women's World Banking

at: womensworldbanking.org

"Gender equality is a spiritual, moral, ethical, social, and economic global sustainability imperative."

AM Owens

Please Review!

All independent authors depend upon reviews left on Amazon.com by readers to help promote their books. Without these reviews, they will hardly get any notice. Please take the time to leave a short review. Simply go to the online bookstore, find the book and go to the book's page. Under the author's name will be a list of reviews and stars. Click here and there will be a big button saying "Create your own review". Please click there and review.

It only takes a minute!

www.ingramcontent.com/pod-product-compliance
Lightning Source LLC
LaVergne TN
LVHW010023070426
835508LV00001B/27